The Witness

Rob Jackson

Thank you to all my soul family

THE WITNESS

INTRODUCTION

Witnessing, as it is written about it in this book, is a form of memory. To witness is to remember that, right now, at this moment, there is nothing that needs to happen. Remembering this frees us up to follow pristine inspiration. This is what is meant when we say that the heart goes first with the mind in tow. We follow inspiration. We notice resonance. We hang out and witness whatever life has brought to us, not making anything of it, just meeting it where it is and responding accordingly. It is a place of pure being, of resting in awareness of what is. It is a following of the subtle urges of the heart and a fearless meeting with heartbreak and setbacks as they come. The Witness is one who can hold it all without being taken by it. The Witness, then, is awareness of an undisturbed presence.

This book should be considered as a work of art, but it is art that is meant to inspire a deeper contemplation of the human condition. There are three parts to this work, each being distinct but connected.

The first is called The Witness, and is a series of short stories that describe a character, The Witness, as it grows through several stages and experiences. The Witness is not a person, although it takes many forms, including that of the human. The Witness is a name for pure awareness, or beingness, as it looks out on the play of forms.

The second part is called The Elements. This section uses story and poetic verse in an attempt to convey the various feeling tones encountered as we move through life. It is meant to stir up and evoke different aspects of these tones within the reader, and to inspire further contemplation.

The third part is called The Code and is a series of meditations on the nature of beingness. The reader is encouraged to move slowly through this section, contemplate the many questions posed, and try some of the suggested exercises.

If there is any truth in this work, I encourage you to hold it as though you discovered it from within yourself. Find it as a living truth rather than as words on a page. If there is resonance with the concepts contained herein, follow up on that resonance. Give it attention and breath and let it grow from within you, that you might become the embodiment of these principles. That your example might shine like a torch for all those in your life who could use some inspiration.

May you take wing,
And fly into the parts of the sky
That are secret and beautiful.

May you find peace,
And settle into the parts of your soul
That are dark and mysterious.

PART ONE

THE WITNESS

CONTENTS

EMERGENCE

He crawled up through the broken blocks of form with all the vigor of a new sprout springing forth into the fresh air of open space. Having a new place for seeing and a new space for expanding, he was glad. He said,

"I now can see all that was previously hidden. But my roots keep me from going too far from here. It seems I can only grow up and out, so I will stay here and put all my energy into my own growth. It was this that allowed me to break through into a new realm of seeing. To go inward, feel my potential, drink in the natural resources around me, and then to give expression to the hidden potential of my DNA. The code for my expansion is written there. Now that I have achieved some growth, I resolve to continue investing my energies into expressing these latent gifts."

He grew and grew, achieving new heights of seeing. The world became plainly visible from these heights. A myriad of colors, a symphony of sounds, a play of tremendous sensation. After some time he spoke again,

"For this growth, I am grateful. I'm held by all the natural elements: the soil, the sun, the rain. My giving is a reinvesting of the energy I've been given, back into my unfolding. I rise through faith since I trust the code that is written within me. I rise through grace since it has not yet failed me."

He continued to grow until he had reached heights at which one could marvel. And from those heights, he could see all that this world contained. He saw the comings and goings. The strivings and surrenders. The empties and the filled. He saw the frightened and the ignorant. The safe and the scared. He saw all the forms this world could produce. From this place of seeing, he spoke again,

"I would stand now, fulfilled in my own growth, and aware of the entanglements of this world. I am grateful for my treasures, the code written within me and the faith that carries this process through. I stand with no clear purpose but to stand. I drink in nourishment with no clear purpose but to be fulfilled. If I would ask who am I, I would find no clear answer. I am the witness of this life unfolding. Perhaps that is all. Perhaps that is enough."

The Witness, he called himself, stood towering over the entanglements of life here. He stood among the bramble, scraped and gauged by the thorns of duality, but only at his lower levels. For in his fullness he reached far beyond the hedges of duality. You could say he extended into a new dimension of awareness. All by reading, hearing, and heeding the calls of the very code written within him.

EXTENSION

As the Witness grew taller, he began to produce fruits and flowers and things. Of his creations, or rather, extensions, some would have wings. His winged fruits would glide upon release, floating along the jet streams and currents of air.

One day, a newly birthed fruit took wing, floating and gliding her way to far off lands, ready to find a spot to settle in and take root. For she had the same code in her as her source, the Witness. And she knew her potential to grow tall like him.

But this strange land was inhospitable to growth. The harsh conditions made it more challenging, and she wondered if the air would ever be pure enough for her to emerge from beneath the soil. For now, the clouds and fog prevented the light from getting through to her. She lamented,

"Here I am in full innocence and preparedness. I have settled into the soil and am ready for my sprouting. But I am dormant here until the light of the sun calls me forth. His calls are muffled in the dreary mists of dreamers, the ones who push me down deeper into the soil. Their hearts call me forth, but their minds heed not their hearts. How long am I fated to remain here unexpressed?"

For many generations, the fog would not lift. And the seeds of the Witness could not take root in this land where the sun was deemed a danger, and the grounds were shielded from its light. But there came a time when the peoples of this place, depressed and malnourished, began to rethink their strategies. And it was this generation that ushered in a miracle- the fog began to lift, and the light was once again allowed to reach the ground. Our seed had stayed patient all this time,

"It would appear the time has come for me to rise and spring forth with all the freshness of new life. I'm blessed to be here with this generation, for the air is dressed with their hope and belief in potential. My eyes have not yet formed, and yet I feel it all around me and have joined them in their hope. And now, together we will co-enable my emergence as the Witness."

Her growth process would not be without its pains since the people of this land were still only learning how to let the light through. But she trusted in the code written within her, like her source, the DNA that had mapped out all she needed. This made her growth even more astonishing and beautiful. With limited light and dusty factions fighting to preserve the old ways, she emerged, the Witness, with a 360 gaze like an ancient goddess. She said,

"I am awareness, afloat and transfixed. I am light embodied. The comings and goings of this world are distant and dim, even as those men clamor for my death. As awareness, my role is to witness. As the Witness, my role is to follow my code to its completion."

EXPANSION

As the Witness expanded, he grew higher and higher, reaching heights that were incomprehensible to those down below. He grew so tall that he penetrated into deep space, beyond the atmosphere of this place. His roots far below remained intact, so his awareness of all levels was not affected. But in this new space, he marveled,

"My seeing is once again elevated in a way that I couldn't have predicted. All the days until now, I have been caught up in the comings and goings of the people below. True, only as a witness, but they still had all of my attention. Now that I can see into deep space, I am beginning to fathom what I assumed to be unfathomable. My awareness stretches farther than the immediate observable happenings of a world in motion. I can see into the abyss of boundless space, and I am awed by a beauty and power of which I was previously unaware."

From that day, many times our Witness would become detached and even disinterested in the hustle he saw around him on the plane of doing. His roots remained well intact, and his awareness of the doer was clear. But having peered into something beyond, his heart was opened. Before he was only aware of the comings and goings of the people. But now, his witnessing enveloped them and extended to something beyond. He remarked,

"I am here, and I am beyond here. The witnessing presence that I am is more than a candle and torch for the wayfarers below. I extend to a boundless dimension where time has been displaced, and doing has become pure being. Now that I have seen this reality, it is seeping through into all my witnessing. No matter what level I perceive, the awareness of boundless being is with me. It is in me, and therefore it is in all I see."

The people did not notice any difference in the Witness. For his role was ever the same. But from that time, his witnessing became something very different. It was more full, more complete, and it was ripe with forgiveness. Having peered into the boundless dimensions, the Witness could hold no grievance. And holding no grievance, his witnessing bestowed a blessing on all those he gazed upon.

CLEARING I

It's true that many beings would seek visitation from the Witness. They bid her come and bless them with her anchored presence. They suspected that, with her 360 gaze, she could see more than any other being. And they expected that from her expanded seeing would follow the words they needed to hear. They would begin by resting and settling into a receptive state before calling her forth. She was kind, and if she sensed that they were of pure intent, she would answer.

One such instance, a king called upon her, worn and tattered from the weights of his worldly duties. She responded to him in quiet,

"Good sir, you have called for a witness, one who is impartial and benevolent, to assess your actions and dispense wisdom. You call for insight, and so I give you this: make space for your secret self to be expressed. The one you hide in the depths of your heart. Go slow and begin to open this space for others to witness. In doing so, you will find me there, immediate and full as though pregnant with a thousand potentials."

He responded by countering her with tales of his own evil. For he had sent men to their deaths, he had run merchants into ruin, he had made life hard for many in the name of the greater good. He thought that surely revealing his secret self meant to expose the hidden evil within him.

"Is there any person who has committed no harm? Is there even a single one here who could claim to be wholly pure? To be revealed, in your case, means to allow others to know your heart of hearts. The place where you are neither born nor die. If you are worried you may be evil, that is the evidence enough that you are not. An evil person would not carry this worry."

The king wept upon hearing this. It was the first time in many years that he had felt into this part of himself. And from his heart began to emerge a new sprout of witnessing, planted in him that night by our Witness.

CLEARING II

On another occasion, an ailing boy called upon her. He was hurt from heartbreak, and frail from a weakened body. His mother had passed away recently, and he was losing interest in his worldly duties. Unsure of himself, he called for her help in sorting out what he was to do. She heard him call in earnest, and from her compassion, she spoke to him,

"Young one, you have requested a salve for a wounded heart, but this I cannot give you. You have sought out advice on what you should do next with your life, I'm sorry to say, I can't give you this either. My role, my function, is as a witness. I notice all and stop for none. In doing so is my blessing bestowed. So be seen, young one, open yourself to me and be witnessed in your fullness. Mourn, if that is what you need. Let loose those uncried tears so that you may imbue yourself with a sound presence."

The young man's heart was dulled, and he could not feel the Witness in her words. He slumped down further into his lamentation, being so young and having to face so much adversity. The Witness spoke again saying,

"I stand at ready, young one, and will be ever-present for when you would call upon me. I will settle in and rest just behind your eyes for when you're ready to turn your gaze inward. I'll be in the soil beneath your numbness for when you are ready to begin feeling again. The soil there is rich with emotion. Come in your time, and meet me at your readiness."

The young one turned and went back sleep. For his young and wounded heart had not yet found its strength.

CLEARING III

There was an occasion when a woman of status called on the Witness. She was an heiress possessed of refinement and taste. She needed no one to support her and trusted her own senses over the advice of others.

But she was plagued by a frequent emptiness and search for purpose. Her burden was one that only manages to surface in a lucky few. In the depths of her darkness, she questioned: what am I even here for? What is the point of this existence? Our Witness was most enticed, and arrived overflowing with verse,

"Hello, my darling. I visit you now as appreciation and fulfillment. Few are those who will pause long enough to let this question surface within them. Fewer still will remain in the burn of this inquiry long enough to see it through. But I have found you full of determination, and so worthy of my presence. Let your determination be for your own seeing. Use it to sharpen your vision that you could pierce the veil of limited understanding. These forms have no purpose because they are transient and fragile. But your being is unassailable and the source of all truth and beauty. Let your determination be to see this truth behind the illusion of forms. Find that which is alive in you that was not born, and will not die."

Upon receiving this insight, the heiress was left speechless. She sat in silence, reflecting upon what seemed like an impossible notion. The Witness spoke again,

"If you would know this for yourself, you must become a witness like me. The Witness does not forsake forms, but she can plainly see her life beyond them. You are here, yes, but here is immense beyond the limits of a mind's understanding. All forms are dead, and yet they are seen to be full of a life that is not their own. Contemplate this, and let us grow together as one, a field of witnessing."

On this night, another Witness emerged from the broken blocks of form.

FULFILLMENT

By now, many millions of witnesses had been born. They were all of unique form and expression. They were all of the same DNA. They grew from each other and for each other. Every corner of every land, from the mountains to the deserts to the forests, the Witness was there. And the sea, from the crests of its waves to its deepest trenches, the Witness was there too. For it had pierced through to deep and boundless spaciousness. It had discovered its rootedness in dimensions that the formed mind couldn't grasp. And so it came to know itself beyond form and beyond the mind. As pure being, knowing, the Witness. Shifted from doer to being, from knower to seeing. A free-flowing, full sea of presence. Unattached to whatever was arising, and yet lovingly holding it all.

But even still, the Witness subjected herself to the full spectrum of experience. The pain of separation, the joy of union. The bitterness of being forgotten, and the relief of being remembered. From hurt to wholeness and everything in between, our Witness came to see life from every conceivable angle. It was this it had come for- to know itself completely and thoroughly. To learn first hand if there were any forms that could disrupt its beingness. So with eyes wide open, she went into every dark corner of every conceivable possibility. She reflected,

"I'm here now, reading about myself as myself. Wondering about myself as myself. I've never left this moment, and yet space and time continue to move all around me. The flux and flow of formed things has not affected my most essential quality-being. I rest now as self-knowing, spacious and unafraid. Empty of worldly worries, and full of divine conviction.

What a marvel, these infinite forms and pathways. I see

myself in all of them. I see myself here, in these words, and in the minds of those interpreting them. I've become the simplest expression of me: I simply am, and in this knowing, all other questioning withers."

The multitude of worlds was left to unfold, as the Witness was anchored in self-knowing. She looked out upon these worlds and watched a trillion forms colliding and suffusing each other with borrowed energies. Everything seemed perfectly in place, exactly as it was.

PART TWO

THE ELEMENTS

Contents

THE FORMS

These are my roots:
Lava pools deep underground,
Branches caressing clouds
On hilltops, and
Wide-eyed creatures
Holding fast to Momma's back

TEARS OF JOY

The flower sheds a tear-
Its petal falls to the ground.

The bittersweet scent of crumbling and dying slowly
Echoes the impermanence of this world.

But if the flower's beauty is lost to decay,
It is found again in its gracious surrender.

For the ground loves sprouting new life,
But delights most when its child returns to it.

NICE AND EASY

I have seen turtles in the water.
They can only stay under for a time
Before they must return again to the surface,
Even if only to peek their head out slightly.

I have seen them sunning on logs.
Resting and soaking in the vibrancy of the sun's light,
But never lacking in vigilance,
Since they won't let me pet them!

These turtles have enviable qualities-
They keep a pace that perfectly matches
Their rhythms, moving about steadily,
They never get ahead of themselves.

THE WOLF

I am not myself when I hate.
I become as though a wound
In need of healing.
But I remember that even the mighty wolf must
Gently lick her wounds to heal them.
So I become the wolf,
Addressing you tenderly.

ILLUMINATED ONE

There you are, shining.
Your beauty comforting me through the darkness of night.
I turned to you
And caught a reflection of myself-
What brilliance you radiate.

Oh, moon, your beauty calls me forth
And bids me come to you.
But you know that I cannot,
So in your generosity you come to me
As light, showing me the path hidden by night.
As the painter, giving life to a canvas of darkness.

You've taught me much, oh moon:
That the prevalence of darkness is no excuse not to shine.
That when viewed in the right light,
a barrier will become a canvas.
That, though unnoticed or unappreciated,
I must shine on anyway.
And to endure the darkness, for I may not
Reach my fullness in just one night.

You have taught my teachers
And will teach my students,
So you have come to represent the Timeless,
Reflecting light from its very source.
The forgotten song you sing reminds me
I am like you.

Natural Reflections

One night, a young soul walked alone in the countryside desiring space and calm. She looked for nothing, so many things were revealed. And not having anything to say, there was much she could hear.

She walked along the edge of the forest, where she saw life in a tree. They studied each other a moment, before the tree spoke to her, saying,

"Greetings, young one. I've stood here many seasons waiting for you. And now you've come and shown me a reflection of myself. It is no coincidence that we are so alike, as we exist both seen and unseen. Like you, my hidden roots keep me firmly grounded that I may reach freely for the sky. My hidden roots keep me nourished and watered. Indeed, even as the fruit falls, it would not be so without these roots."

The young soul thanked the tree for its wise reflections, feeling the gratitude deep into her own roots, where the tree's wisdom had landed.

She continued walking and saw ahead a mountain stream tumbling along its way. As she drew nearer, the stream saw its reflection in her, and began serenading her with a lullaby that satiated her thirsting spirit,

"Young soul, welcome to my place of worship. I have waited to meet another like me, one who could hear my song. Have you noticed our resemblance? Like you, I too am ever flowing towards those junctures when I both meet and lose myself in a larger stream. Flowing forcefully when waters are high, and meekly when waters are low, I continue to flow unbothered. For I waste no time to measure my river-ness. I am content to flow

24

until my waters have rejoined the ocean."

Our young soul bowed in gratitude and wiped at her moistened cheeks. To be witnessed by such natural beauty is no small thing.

Barely had she taken another step when from below her feet the stone would be overlooked no longer, and spoke to her, saying,

"Hello, young one! I'm happy to meet another friend like me. Perhaps one day we can both be the foundation for a temple. Don't you find that many pass you by, as to them, we seem rather ordinary? But perhaps there is some ancient treasure hidden deep within us. Waiting patiently to be rediscovered by those who care to examine more carefully."

The young soul pressed her feet down and stood up tall, feeling emboldened by the boulder's thoughtful verse. She knew he had seen her all the way through, and had offered his sturdy support.

As she walked on, she found a clearing on a grassy hill and sat down to watch the sky. From above, a lively moon found a break in the clouds. Looking out on her it said,

"Oh joy, another one like me has met my gaze. I celebrate our sameness, young one, for like you I have one half reflecting a magnificent light, penetrating and dissolving darkness, while the other half is in complete darkness awaiting its time in the light. But have you noticed how both sides know by now to be patient?"

Tears again dressed her cheeks as the moon's song found her open heart and poured itself in, closing the divide of otherness.

And there she sat on the hill, listening to the wondrous harmonies of nature all around. They all came together with one heart and one voice, singing the hymn of the living:

"It is I, the Spirit behind form,
I have directed my infinite particles to organize, and
Now that I am in motion,
I am both the formed and the formless,
I am an ocean searching my own mysterious depths,
I am the blind using my hands to discern beauty,
Indeed, I am a mystery discovering itself!"

As our young soul descended the hill to make her return to the village, she noted the silence that had accompanied her during her walk. And she resolved to keep this companion close to her forever more. She danced and laughed her way home with a full heart, thankful for what had been revealed in the darkness of night.

THE MYSTERY

The simple, the subtle,
The vast depth of unknowing,
I bow to you

For Science

A process called dissection
Has left this child whole.
For only now do I truly know myself,
After being cut open and put on display
For any and all who cared
To see what's inside me.

It was after this careful examination
That I made my most important discovery-
None of these forms contains me.

STILL RHYTHMS

The rhythm of stillness is
A beating heart
Radiating electric waves of color
And sound.
Soft waves that wrap up forms and
Suffuse spaces.

The rhythm of stillness is carried
On these waves.
Holding the center,
The origin point of all sound and color,
Stillness permeates outward.

I'm all in on it since,
Put to good use,
This rhythm unlocks
New dimensions of knowing.

THE SECRET PATH

The secret path, the one that brings us to paradise.
To that secret spot where no one has to sacrifice.

The secret path isn't actually much of a secret.
It never bothers to hide itself,
But still the people mostly don't notice it.

By slowing down and really noticing what's here,
By pausing our doing, our efforting to get somewhere,
This path is revealed.
It shows itself upon the death of either-or thinking.

To take the secret path is
To accept the gift with open hands.
To receive insight with an open mind.
To deny the urge to believe our choices are limited.

The secret path is always a gift.
It gifts us with humility.
It's the stone falling from the sky
That cracks open our glass ceilings.

Where does it fall from?
Who knows, just say thank you
And take the path when it opens.
And give a humble acknowledgment to
The Muse who tossed the stone.

SELF-KNOWING

It's a juicy offer, to know thyself
By comparison. We humans are always striving to
Know ourselves, eh?
We ask, what am I anyway?
Am I good, am I bad?
Am I near, am I far?
Am I good right here, or
Should I move over there?
There's an acute pain to the uncertainty, like
A splinter in the palm or
A bitten lip, a nagging hurt just
Loud enough to keep us from being able to overlook it.
I must know-
What is my standing?

I think this urge to know ourselves by comparison
Is a cover for a deeper urge-
To know that we are loved.
To trust that we are held.
To trust that, in this moment,
I am enough.

THE DOORWAY

What door is there
That doesn't lead to another door?
Even entry into the sanctuary
Is meant to lead one to
The door of the soul.
Even the door to the soul
Is meant to lead one into
Timeless Presence.

But what door is there that
Could lead to omniscience?
What door is there that
Could lead to unhindered expansion?
What door is there that
Could lead to right here?

If I walk through doors,
I'll always be walking through doors.
If I stay right here,
I'll always be open, here.
If I'm always open, what need have I for doors?

THE SHADOW

A shadow is cast when belief
Stumbles in front of light,
And space stagnates from
Breath constrained

DUNGEON DELVING

I dive deep into the wound
To hold space for my own healing.

I found the judger here, sat on a
Throne of bones, living in a dungeon,
Confused, believing he runs the kingdom.

WHISPERING PHANTOMS

The devil hides in the shadows
Ever elusive, and yet persistent
In his whisperings.

I cry those shadows into light,
but he's nowhere to be found.
Only to be heard speaking on
Fear from another shadow.

When I bring that shadow to light,
He is again gone with no trace.

I'm beginning to think
He was never there at all.

SHAME

Anger and discontentment-
My secret house guests.
And yet I try to shoo them out the back door
When my more pleasant guests arrive.

The Prescription

Police, prescribe, push over a ledge,
Sovereign knowing is lost on the head,
The mind it thinks, therefore thinks it knows,
From this assumption all violence flows,
All loss and theft and heartburning pain,
Since only a mind could think it's separate,
So it polices, prescribes, and pushes around,
Thinking the path it thinks it found
Can make it whole again

PREDICTABLE SMALLNESS

Craving the familiar is a net in which
Many are caught.
Wanting what we know we want.
Going where we've enjoyed going.
Familiar energy fields producing
Familiar sensations of lightness, heaviness.
Revolving doors of thought-
Always moving in a new direction
Without having to go anywhere.

Such a safe feeling even though
It eats us alive from the inside since
There's no soul satiation in repeating patterns,
In predictable smallness.
Craving the familiar,
The soul probably does this to die, having been
Tricked into believing in some littleness about itself.
And little things die, though they
Fight to stay alive.

A soul is never satisfied with smallness
And would rather feign death than to stay
Where it can't stretch out and admire its own fullness.

DISCRIMINATION

Beauty is all life.
But to behold it can be overwhelming,
So we close our mind's eye,
And discriminate.

The tragedy is that we don't see
Our blindness is so easily remedied.
But a long closed eye will need a gentle
Pry to open again.

GOOD COMPANY

If the sky rained tears, I wonder
Who would notice?
If the sky rained blood, not one
Of us would miss it.
The laws of nature lift to the sky
Neither the blood of the fallen
Nor the tears of the grief-stricken.
Only water falls from the sky, and
It washes away both blood and tears into the
Mud underfoot.

But pain isn't invisible and
Trauma not easily forgotten.
So I wonder, will we outlast our memories?
I wonder if, when the curtain falls on this play,
Will we all celebrate together?

WAR

Into the woods, deep into the night,
Visibility is gone for now.
The living fall into a river of blood, and
The tide rises higher.
But this the soil cannot drink, instead
She chokes and sputters while
I stand in her dark forest, naked and invisible.

I am afraid because I cannot see,
I am afraid, so I do not speak.
My heart is torn so profusely bleeds,
But the soil rejects my offering.
I've nowhere to climb and I dare not fall,
So my next recourse: tear down this wall.
Erected in front as machines push from behind,
The seeds of hate take root in my mind.
Planted by trembling and desperate hands,
Perhaps I am the devil, or at least his hands,
Now watch as I destroy my fellow man.

The Empire and The Priest

In the time of empires and battlefields, there was a land that had prospered for many generations. An ominous time came upon this empire in the form of a new foe that they could not overcome. In a single battle, they lost their most famous and loyal warriors. When the news reached the capital city, many would not believe it, deeming it hearsay proliferated by the enemy. Others though were overcome with fear and began to flee the city.

There was a beloved priest in this land. When he heard the news of the lost battle, he knew it to be true. The city's favorite champion had sought him out for questioning only a few days before the fighting began.

On this day, the priest sat with his chaplains holding sanctuary in their temple while the city descended into turmoil. Many were afraid and asked the priest to address them. He spoke, saying,

"My dearest companions, fellow lightkeepers, be not afraid in these tumultuous times. We have remained here in this dark land to be a light for the downtrodden, and to hold sanctuary for the devotional. We have remained in proximity to all those carrying on with wars and refusing to acknowledge Spirit. They are like a flower that does not comprehend the sun and deems days to be good fortune and nights to be bad luck. Unhindered, the sun shines and asks nothing from us but our own growth, and the giving of our fruits back to the earth.

"This empire has been like an invasive plant overtaking a garden, and still the sun has fed it well and good. The sun does not discriminate, though his earth-child sometimes grows unsavory things. He loves what some might call weeds, and distributes His light evenly to us all.

"The champion whom this city loved met with his darkened fate. For at the dusk of his life was found the dawning of his self-knowledge. Just days before he left for his campaign, he sought me out for questioning. The dogma of patriotism had worn thin. He was unsure of his purpose and had grown tired of fighting.

"When he was with me, I studied his pained expression and watched as the weight of his might wore on him. The strongest among us seem to don the heaviest loads. But I tell you, it is only because of their load that they seem to be the strongest. I said to him,

'War is always ugly. It is an affront to the holy truth seared into our hearts. When you take up arms, you are one hand moving to strike the other. Every blow struck lands to your larger self. Indeed, you are the wind-blown seed taking up root in the neighbor's garden. You take but from yourself.

'Brave champion, you fight for an empire of the heartless. They overtook this garden centuries ago. They called their weeds flowers and deemed their overgrowth to be abundance. Now comes the next invasive plant to overtake it again. And this one who is standing across from you in battle is but another plant in God's garden.'

"And with that, the warrior left from me in haste, not saying a word. His inquiry was an omen of what was to come. I can only pray that he felt complete with his role in the play before exiting the stage.

"You, my dearest friends, have come for the same, have you not? Half the city flees while the other half stands frozen in disbelief. It appears now that this empire will fall. But falling is no bad thing. For we always fall into the soil from which we arose, and those who fall shall rise again tomorrow in the form of something new. Like the sun, we have a cycle we are obligated to keep. Fear not the approaching night. Remember that a candle of faith will do until the sun again rises."

When the priest finished his address, they went together to the balcony to watch the sunset. They each contemplated in silence what it meant to fall. All the monuments erected by the empire would soon be like dust and settle into the dirt underfoot. All the peoples would be displaced and scattered like seeds to the wind. They found strength in each other, and the knowing within their hearts. Each held tight his candle of faith. And they heard the priest's soft singing,

"Be like the water
Flowing towards a fall,
So that we may bear witness to
The beauty of your letting go."

THE FIRE

Here fall the tears of
The bodhisattva,
Whatever forms they wash away
Turn to ash

THE CUTTING EDGE

I like to dance and play in places I could never stay.
Like running down a slant,
It's too late to stop or slow down.
The momentum has me,
And I'm surrendered to the rhythm.
My rhythm
Punches through stagnant space like a drum,
Synchronizing hearts and bodies
Into a seamless, singular expression
Of movement and sound,
And together we become as one voice,
As one holy Yes.

So far all those who relate, hear my call.
You know who you are,
That one who creates new pathways.
We are the cutting edge,
Existing as electrified potential.
We're the mounting pressure that throws lava into the sky.
We're the first measure of a new refrain.
We've come to dance,
And throw our heads back in raucous laughter.
We've come to disturb and disrupt and make messes.
We've come to play,
And let our voices rise to soaring heights.
We've come to stumble and stutter
And get mud on our good shoes.
We've come to dance and play
In places we know we won't stay.
We're just passing through,
We're the cutting edge.

The Witness

We carry the very thing our hearts have been clamoring for-
The potential for springs of new life,
The breath of fire that singes the lingering and lazy,
The eyes alit with purpose and clarity,
The forms on fire with a willingness to serve.
And to serve a purpose that we may not fully grasp,
But we feel its invisible influence.

Let us embody this invitation for all those
Who lay eyes on us:
Come and play in the light of your own fiery heart!
Can you feel it now?
It's yours forever

BIGNESS

I wish these things for you:

Find your arms that are
Big enough to hold the devil.

Feel your heart soft enough
To enfold the dagger.

Look with eyes that are clear enough
To see the light in dark disguises.

Stand with feet strong enough
To stay rooted in the storm.

And courage!
Have courage enough to believe in your own goodness.

In your Bigness there is no one bigger than you.
In your Bigness you extend to envelop the whole of it-
No concept stands over you,
And no idea encompasses you.

Stand your ground.
Hold your space.
We're here with you.

BE BRAVE

Summon your courage,
And step into the fire.
Give yourself to its magnetic beauty.
The fire delights to dance in the night,
And to warm the weary and downtrodden.

But still its purpose must be
To consume some part of you,
Until all that remains is a blank canvas
So that each day may paint something new upon it.

Later, after all has been burnt,
You have been sufficiently purified,
And the flame has cooled,
Spread the ashes into the soil,
And plant your garden there.

REBELS

"A little bit of rebellion is a good thing,"
Said the flower growing from a crack in the pavement.

"A little bit of defiance can be good,"
Said the broken heart protecting its wounds.

"We're not going against anyone,"
They say together,
"We're just claiming our territory."

SINGLE-POINTEDNESS

A famous warrior happened through a usually quiet town. He was well known in the region for his many exploits during battles in nearby lands. His armor and spear shown like rare treasures, sparkling in the midday sun. The people of the village were abuzz to know he was among them.

An assembly of eager admirers formed near the markets, marveling at the stature and presence of this warrior. They asked him to speak and desired to know the source of his strength. He took a moment to reflect, before saying to them,

"My spear and I are as one whole system. My body is extended and my power amplified with this tool in hand. When I advance, I proceed from behind the single point at the spear's tip, since it is here that I am sharpest and penetrate most deeply."

A man asked, "What of us whom have no spear and cannot fight? We would be great too!"

The warrior paused, taking in the eager eyes encircling him before replying,

"I have my tools, and you have yours. The tool has no life unto itself, it has no inherent value. It can amplify power but has none of its own.

So I would ask, what are your sharpest and sturdiest tools? Is it your voice, your hands, your hammer? Is it your feet, your brush, your threads? Whatever tools you carry, understand that they may extend you, but do not contain you. They may amplify you, but they are not a source of power unto themselves.

Just as your body extends your mind, so do your tools extend your body. They are not separate parts- mind, body, tool- they are as one whole.

Just as you strengthen your body, so too must you sharpen your tools. Just as you expand your mind, so too must you grow your repertoire. If you would be great in your trade, contemplate this."

The crowd became quiet, and the warrior went on his way.

WARRIOR SPIRIT

If Love knows no bounds,
Then neither will I.
Now I stand in stillness,
Feeling the power of a beating heart,
This is all the confidence I need.

Hate, indifference, suffering-
I'm coming for you.

THE HEART

At the tender union of
Spirit and creature,
Of Heaven and Earth,
A heart is born to love

WARWICK GOBLE.

TAKE A MOMENT

This moment is yours for the taking.
Pause and breathe,
This moment is free-
Please take it.

Go slow,
    or fast,

Be big,
    or small,

Whatever you need.
This moment is yours.

AMPLE STORES

Be generous with love;
Its supply is inexhaustible.
Its source is immutable,
And its impact is often invisible.

Be generous with love; it's the
Only thing there is an infinite supply of.

If I can't find any within me to give,
It's because I have turned away from God's storehouse.
I have tried to grow my own crops in darkness.
Not to worry though,
Today I will mourn my vain efforts,
And return back to the village that love built.
Because my heart is in a clamor,
Longing only to have some love to give,
Longing to be the most generous lover.

The Prescription Cont'd

Police, prescribe, push over a ledge,
The way to be right, for the
Thought-strewn head.

Relax and witness, give all to my part,
For I am whole, sings
The love-full heart.

A Tender Truth

We've been here for a while now,
Dancing from star to star.
It's the love in our hearts
That got us tangled up lifetimes ago.
An entanglement of hearts that never lets go.
And since it happens in the heart, a tender truth
Is revealed-
That we are a reference to the love of God.

Tender as it is, it's impenetrable like the darkest night.
Sturdy as it is, it's fluid like the free form dancer.
Free as it is, it's slave to the will of the Holy.
Devoted as it is, dogma has no place to enter.
Grand as it is, it's expressed in subtle gestures.
Tender as it is, it knows only invulnerability.

This tender Truth, resounding and thorough,
Got us tangled up lifetimes ago.
A sweet, eternal verse, a hum of silence,
Beckoning us back to here and now.
Revealing that which our hearts have always known,
That I am.

BELOVED

You have inspired me
And helped awaken an ancient yearning.
I beheld it in you
And could not utter a word
That properly expressed my feeling.

BELOVED II

In you I would seek the meaning of life,
And in you I would find myself.
For the beckoning of your love
Echoes Infinity.

Beloved III

My longing for you is my longing for love.
The beauty with which you mesmerize me
Is the beauty of all Life,
For you embody these elements
Like no other I can perceive.

REVELATION

I wish I could show you who you really are.
I wish I could pull back a dozen veils to reveal your heart.
All of life springs from there.
All the simple truths fall into place there.
I wish I could give you an experience of wholeness,
Of being complete and full.
I wish you could meet me here, right now.
I wish my heart had legs and could come to you,
And arms to wipe the dust from your eye.
I wish I could show you who you really are,
Underneath all those dusty layers of identity.
God's Child lives there, in that heart.
Pristine and undisturbed.
Golden and whole.

I wish you knew who you really are,
So you could meet me as that.
So that we could look each other in the eye
Joining again like we never left
The unified field, the healed heart,
A web spun from intention laced with infinity.
I wish I could show you who you really are,
Right now, in words.

Perhaps you'll see past these forms,
And feel my heart in them.
Then we can show each other who we really are.
Whole and complete with nothing left out,
No one left aside.
And we can offer each other our most holy prayer:
Hi

As You Are

I thought I could speak to you,
    That my words might impart wisdom.

I thought I could show you,
    That my example might inspire action.

I thought I could encourage you,
    That my nudging might set you in motion.

It was all this thinking that obscured my knowledge.
I became wise when I accepted that I could
Never move you from where you are in this moment.
I could only welcome you as you are.
In this way, there is nothing between us, and we have
Joined in what is. This one act is so powerful that
The impact reverberates throughout the heavens.

NOW I BECOME LOVE

Now I become Love,
Stirrer of souls.

Now I become Love,
Spring of truth.

Now I become Love,
Visage of light.

Now I become Love,
Unbroken whole.

Love is not a force,
Love is all there is.

Love isn't all we need,
Love is all we are.

Love is the natural result,
Love is the certain outcome,
Love is the undisturbed I Am-ness
Resting beneath all forms.

THE DREAM

I dream of spring,
I dream of rivers,
I even dreamt that I was dreaming
Someone else's life

A Visitor

In a strange land I am a visitor,
But what is this faint familiarity that suggests
I have been here before?

Perhaps in a dream I met my host.
We spoke the same tongue,
Danced the same steps,
And were similarly adorned.

In this dream we fell in love,
Our hearts merging into one center.
Our minds knew we could not stay,
But our full hearts met bravely with separation.

We awoke into another dream,
Our sleepy imaginings drifted off.
But upon waking I began following my heart,
And it led me here, back to you
In this strange land.

GREAT WAVES

Sat still, I begin to ponder
The mysteries that I may find
With a heart allowed to wander
Free from the many fears that bind

I drift into a deeper space,
For I would know my own depth,
There's something here time can't erase
A treasure my heart has kept

At surface the master is time,
But does something more lie beneath
Familiar dimensions of mind?
What mysteries dwell in waters deep?

Thoughts and feelings arrive like waves
Upon my shores, then back to the sea,
Delivering that which I crave,
They get along fine without me

Waves exist but on the surface,
Deep currents remain their dictate,
And the wave ponders not purpose,
Neither is she heard to curse fate

Collapse is the wave's destiny
Going peacefully and with grace,
Knowing its freedom is the sea,
Surrendering to show its faith

Be then I wave or particle?

Are outward shows to be believed?
Dull concepts seeming farcical,
Not knowing becomes my relief

To become the sea, my great wish,
Perhaps someday I will have it,
Or maybe there is truth already in this
While a mind attempts to grasp it

DREAMING IN THE DARK

Ancient memories visit like dreams,
Suggesting that I am asleep.
And how deeply so
That in my dream I remember other dreaming
In far off places.
And how far have I fallen into slumber,
How long I have I tumbled on the edge
Of complete darkness?
It seems impossible to tell.
Have I drifted too far to be redeemed?
Will I remain asleep for all eternity?

A spark of light would be all that is needed,
A brief reminder that the shore is still
Only a few feet away.
That only shallow waters separate me
From the ground of all being.

CHANGING TUNES

Sometimes when I want a thing I ask myself,
What is it that I don't have, that this will bring me?

There are those who soundly know what they desire.
I admire their steadfastness and surety,
And seek to be like them in that way.

There are those who take a careful approach
Before they choose anything.
I admire their patience and confidence,
And seek to be like them as well.

It seems that in the human there must be a balance.
For even as I pursue some object of my desires,
So must I allow my desires to evolve and be refined.
For they too have a life and a journey to make,
A song to sing.

Their song is expressed in my heart, and
I dare not muffle it.

I should not be so certain that I know what I want,
And I should not assume that I do not know.

A Whisper in the Dark

Hello, young one,
Won't you come and enjoy the amenities?
We're here for you.
You've asked us to come and be
A part of this world.
There is none here that you did not call forth,
There is none but the urges of hidden awareness
Evident here.
You reach much further than those little arms.
You travel far beyond even your dreaming of
Ancient places
And curious creatures organizing
According to celestial guides,
Following paths laid out by the ancients.

The evidence is here
Okay, Sherlock? It's not even hiding,
But maybe you are.

Dream Worlds

There was once a young boy who dreamed in unusual ways. He dreamt while awake and going about his day. The images and sounds from his mind were overlaid onto the world around him. Often he was invigorated by his dreams. He could see colors that no one else seemed to notice. He could hear notes that no others responded to. He reflected,

"What a marvelous gift, this ability to dream. My fellow humans must but see life in gray and dull tones. While I see all that and more! On the teacher at school, I dreamt she wore horns on her head and had a tail! And the fireman I saw after class, he could ride his fire hose like it was a giant snake! In the song my mother sings to me at night, I hear a harp more beautiful than the song of angels. I'm just a boy, but with these dreams, I feel I'm special."

Other times though, the dreams were less savory, even downright frightening. His overlays would show him dark images and make harsh noises. In those times, he wished he could be rid of his dreams. He lamented,

"I'm afraid and alone in a world of my own making. These images are ghastly and demonic. I would hide, but I've nowhere to run from the images I'm creating! I curse this dream. Now my desire is only to see things as they truly are."

The child would cycle back and forth like this throughout his adolescence. But as he grew, the dreaming tendencies gradually faded. Over time the images and sounds could not affect him so much. He knew they were coming from his own mind. He knew they were like shadows on a wall. Knowing this, his tendency to dream began to erode.

Later in life after he'd reached maturity, he looked back and reflected,

"I remember those days when I dreamt a world that was not there. I remember well both the exuberance and the terror. An unschooled mind had left me with a perpetual distortion of sight. But I outgrew that old tendency. I've found it more than enough see the truth of things as they are. The simple truth before any dream is laid upon it. Now when I see the young ones reacting to harsh nightmares or basking in sweet dreams, I'm compassionate to their experience. And I let them be with their dreams, all the while knowing that there is a simple beauty to the world underneath all the overlays. But I know too that, in time, they will grow to see it for themselves."

THE MUSIC

The final reveal,
The last layer pulled back
To expose a heart,
Singular and full, springing forth
With song

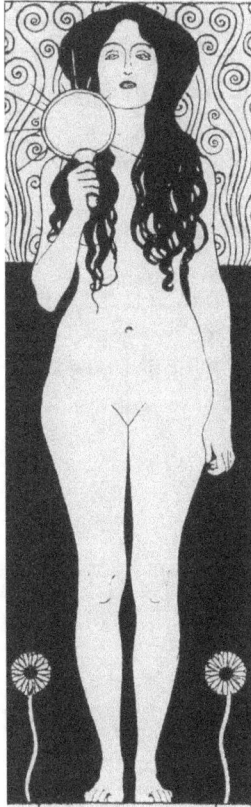

The Jeweler

Go and install your gems upon the world.
The place could use a bit of your shine!
Polish and refine,
Measure and cut,
And when you are ready, reveal your
Priceless treasures for us.

Hang your painting in the halls of society.
Sing your song at the intersections of activity.
Unveil your craft in the marketplace of thought.

Install your gems upon the world, and
From time to time, tend to them.
Let's shine this place up a bit!

The more of us to do it,
The brighter this place will get,
And the easier it'll be for us to see
The truth of things.

HOLD YOUR SPACE

Never be intimidated;
Humility is enough.
Become the always-student-always-teacher,
Observing truthful expression
As it moves from person to person,
Keeping one eye on it always.
If you notice it absent in another,
Be sure it is present in you.

Sing It

A light in the dark,
What a wonder thereof,
To the desperate
A candle will do.

Was it fortune,
Perhaps fate
That delivered to us
The brilliant light within you.

Some call life a journey,
Some call it a ride,
But I see now
That neither is true.

The wind whispered to me
"It's a song, dear boy,
Sung by a heart
In tune."

So if I ever forget that
Gifts are for giving,
I'm gently reminded
By you.

RESTS

Out of the silence many sounds arise.
Why not make music from them?

Pain is one tone, joy is another.
Longing is one, and satisfaction another.

Out of the silence many sounds arise.
For now, let's make music from them.

It is for this we created these feelings,
We believed we could improve upon silence.

The Musician

Show yourself,
And touch some part of me that I can't see.
Remind me that it's there.
Remind me who I am.

DIE TO LIVE

Now I leave
The nest of littleness,
And sing my song
To the world

Now I die
To all the known forms,
And begin my
Life as music

Now I strip
Myself bare,
And reveal my
Naked desire

Now I sink
Into darkness,
And meet with
Invisible being

Now I leave
The nest of littleness,
And become as
Boundless destiny

PART THREE

THE CODE

CONTENTS

HUMAN BEING

Human is the creature of the body. The one who has plans and ideas, the one who carries fear and trauma, and experiences itself as having a distinctly separate life from all other creatures. The human needs ground. It needs breath. It needs other humans to connect with. The human is the one that is just doing its best, even though it can't get things perfect or be whole unto itself.

Being is the timeless quality of life. It is pure life force that is seen to filter through the constructs of the human. Being is not subject to interpretation. It simply is. It is not referential or relative. That is, it doesn't exist relative to something else. It is life underneath all forms. Being is the witnessing presence that is the primary theme of this book.

Being is knowing. Not knowing things, but knowing that I am, that I exist.

Being is creating. Not building or producing, but to lend life to forms.

Being is extending. Not reaching or grasping, not leaning in or leaning out, but to stay in the center and bestow our blessings. This is to extend.

Being is expanding. To extend is to expand because we experience more of ourselves each time we do so.

Being is witnessing. Giving life, extending, is seeing past the veil of forms to the simple innocence of the play of life.

All of this can be summed up like this: to live, to be, is to love. Because to love is to expand. To love is to see past the surface to the simple truth of things. To love is to know that I Am. To love is to join the disparate elements of life back into oneness.

FORMED AND FORMLESS

A form is anything that has a boundary around it. This could include objects, events, concepts, ideas, feelings, and more. Forms act as a temporary host to life. They are vehicles for experiencing.

Our bodies are forms. The thoughts we think are forms. The emotions we feel are forms. The items we make are forms. All forms have a beginning and an end. They are perceived, read, interpreted, held, constructed, and dissipated.

Formlessness is potential. It is the ground of life that exists before any lines of separation are drawn. The formless quality of life is what precedes miracles. We could call it "the unseen." It is always alive, always fresh, always present, and always thrives. It rests pre-perception. It cannot be perceived. The Witness is formlessness gazing upon form. The error occurs when formlessness looks out, believes its perceptions, and temporarily solidifies itself as form. Error, in this context, does not indicate something wrong, but simply a mistake in perception. That the immutable quality of life has been overlooked.

The practice of self-inquiry is a great way to explore formlessness. This practice is about tracing our sense of aliveness to its source, or as close to it as we can get. It could go something like this:

Sit quietly and settle into a relaxed state of mind. Then begin to ask yourself these questions, pausing to reflect after each one:

Who am I that is hearing these thoughts?

Who am I that is noticing these feelings?

Who am I?

Who is asking?

Resist the temptation to answer any of these questions with thoughts or ideas or words of any sort. The answer, if there is to be one, is a direct experience of the pure awareness that is formlessness. And when you have this experience you might ask, who is watching awareness?

If this sort of practice appeals to you, I highly recommend a study of the great teachers of this lineage such as Ramana Maharshi, Nisargadatta Maharaj, and Mooji.

TIME AND TIMELESS

Time as we experience it could be described as the perception of an ongoing series of intervals. Progression, regression, evolution, etc., these are ways of tracking intervals. All changes in form, whether considered good or bad, require an interval. Though change itself appears to be constant.

The perception of intervals frames the linear and spatial levels of experience. For example, there seems to be an interval:

Between past and present,
Between present and future,
From one thought to the next,
Between you and me,
Between person and planet,
From this word to this word.

But what is an interval? Can it be perceived? How is it experienced?

All intervals, whether spatial or in time, are in one way imagined. It is a way for the mind to track life's dynamism. The interval creates a small amount of space for which to insulate an experience on both sides. It is a method of division, and therefore, a child of the parent thought of separation.

Timelessness shows itself when we, if only for a moment, live without the interval. This is the witnessing of life. Without going anywhere, without moving even one inch from the center of being, to stay present and meet fearlessly with whatever arises. Attention has intervals, but the Witness does not. The Witness says, "I am here, always."

A close examination of the interval is a step towards a direct experience of timelessness. A few questions to contemplate are written below. As with the practice of self-inquiry, it is recommended that you do not answer them with words, but rather, pause for a direct experience. Sit with each one for a minute and see what comes up.

What is communication without an interval?

What is the interval between people composed of? Can it be perceived?

What does the interval between myself and nature consist of? How do I know that I am separate from my surroundings?

What of the interval between thoughts? Is it possible to look directly at it?

Intervals are seen to last for an instant. So how long is an instant?

An exercise that could be interesting: sit facing another person, holding eye contact, while both people contemplate these questions. For example, asking oneself, "what does the interval between us consist of?" And notice what happens when we try to look directly at it.

Focus

An unfocused mind is the cause of all manner of difficulties. The mind tends towards distraction, disorganization, and uncertainty. Often we react to this by forcing ourselves to focus, tightly holding the mind to its task. But this can bring other problems since we run the risk of developing tunnel vision.

In contemplating an integrated form of focus, one that is neither too narrow nor too loose, we must consider that the mind requires training to accomplish anything. Training our focus should remain a priority as long as we have a mind running after things.

Consider what it would be like to have a mind that is singularly focused, but its singular focus is broad enough to meet with whatever might arise in the moment. This is called single-pointed focus. To bring the mind to a single point, but in keeping that point large enough to include body awareness, spatial awareness, and awareness of the other beings in the space. To do this requires training.

An exercise to help with this learning:

Hang with another person. Sit facing each other and hold eye contact as best you can. For a few minutes, go back and forth naming what you are noticing. Try to keep your noticings succinct and broad. Some examples could be,

Tension in my legs
Distracting thoughts
Eyes
The light blinking behind you

After a minute or two of this, shift your noticing to your mere presence. For a minute or so, go back and forth noticing that you are here. For example,

I'm here.
Just here.
I'm here.
I am.

Now share with each other what this experience was like. While you share, see if you can hold steady your sense of presence. This is part of the exercise.

Don't push any thoughts or feelings away. The objective of this exercise is to meet with whatever arises without leaving the moment. Leaving the moment means going into analysis, reflection, or survival mode about what is happening. You could say the purpose of this exercise is to develop the capacity for pure noticing, and to stretch awareness so that it becomes flexible and strong.

After a time, when this level of focus becomes more natural, the mind will of its own accord begin to relax and slow down. The key is to be patient. Keep in mind that to witness is to remember that nothing needs to happen. In this way, we are free to love ourselves regardless of what the mind is going on about.

CREATING

To live is to create. Just by being alive, creating happens.

You could say that being and creating are synonymous. We can't live even for an instant without creating. A body is continuously creating at a cellular level. A person is creating when they form sentences, make their bed, nurse their child, hum a song, or caress their lover's body. Every action requires creativity. And every act of creating is unique to the moment.

To introduce the mind to single-pointed focus is a boon to creating since the disciplined mind can better focus its energies.

We are often tempted to think of creativity in limited terms. Or we may even believe that we don't have it. But creating is neither narrow nor can it be covered or destroyed. It is a foundational aspect of being. A person's unique artistry is revealed in their every authentic expression. Artistry here means creative style and ability.

An exercise to try. In a journal, write a few sentences to follow each prompt listed below:

The times I feel most creative are..

My personal style is expressed in..

I feel most inspired when..

These are simple prompts that can help keep us in touch with our sense of creativity, authentic self, and an honest reflection.

GOD-SOURCE

In contemplating God, we can think in terms of cause and effect. The core knowing that I am, that I exist, is called beingness. This essential life force is an effect of God. In other words, God could be considered cause and our essential Self could be considered the effect.

God represents the origination of life, of beingness, while we represent the extension of that life. But we also create alike to our creator, so we are one part extension and one part originator. This is integrated beingness, to acknowledge and bow to Source, while at the same time inhabiting our own power to create.

Countless teachers and philosophers have instructed us through the ages to look within to discover God. I would be no different. On an Egyptian temple you'll find the inscription:

"The body is the house of God." That is why it is said: "Human, know thyself."

Know yourself without any pretext.
Know yourself as a channel for divine creativity.
Know yourself as presence.
Know yourself at your most essential,
And say nothing of what you find to anyone.

HEAVEN

Heaven is not a state or condition, it is an awareness of perfect oneness.

Perfect oneness means infinite communication.

The body is a communication device.

Guilt's only purpose is to disrupt communication.*

Contemplate for a moment what infinite communication would be like. There would be no hashing things out because all parts instantly and always see from every other perspective. So when any one part acts, they do so as a function of a supreme unified will. This is a hint at what an experience of oneness is like. It also gives us a clue about why so many ancient traditions advise us to surrender our individual will to a higher power.

Perhaps our task then, is to nurture clear communication channels with all other beings. And to, with help, release the guilt and fear stored in our bodies and minds that disrupts honest communication.

I wonder, what would it be like to have a completely clear channel of communication with even one other person?

As an exercise, consider a person where there is a lot of charge or judgment being held in mind. Someone that is seen as awful, harmful, or otherwise undesirable. Take a few moments to catalogue your grievances, and let surface those feelings of disgust, anger, or whatever they may be. Then contemplate the following questions.

What is communication like with this one as they are perceived now?

If the channel were clear and open, what would I communicate to them?

What do I think they need to know?

*First section loosely adapted from A Course In Miracles

Prayer

Prayer takes many forms. Its form is not so important. People everywhere have their preferred forms, and all of them have the potential to be useful. What determines their usefulness is how they are held.

If a person comes into prayer with the inward condition of a beggar, their prayers are not likely to yield the desired fruits. A beggar is one who feels or acts impoverished, that is to say, there is not enough of something. The reason this limits prayer's effectiveness is because it bypasses an incorruptible truth of life: that each person has an essential dignity. To understand that I am valuable, not for what I do, but for what I am, is the foundation of dignity.

If a person goes into prayer with an understanding of their inherent value, they will approach prayer much differently. They will understand that their prayer, their voice and intention, have power.

Whether it be meditation, journaling, hiking in nature, eye-gazing with a partner, on bended knee kissing the earth or a thousand other ways. No matter how you pray, do it with dignity. And never yield to the temptation to view yourself as a victim appealing to a savior. You have power! You are a gift. Acknowledge this and pray from that place.

SPIRIT

Spirit is the communication medium that connects us with Source. It is the field from which all forms of intelligence arise. Each piece claims a partial intelligence, while Spirit is the unbroken whole.

Individual identities, all the forms of partial intelligence, are like waves in the ocean of Spirit. Partial intelligence is always temporary because all forms are temporary. It is the destiny of all life to once again merge with the field of unlimited intelligence that is Spirit.

Spirit can never be cut off from Source, just as the person can never be cut off from Spirit. That is to say, a person can never be totally cut off from unlimited intelligence. The boundary we sometimes experience is composed of a belief in limitation, or rather, a lack of faith in the Supreme.

Vision is an essential quality of Spirit. It sees past individuated forms to the life contained therein. It is a recognition of self in other. It is Spirit looking upon Spirit. Therefore, we say:

Perception is a barred window.
Consciousness is an open window.
Vision is going outside.

FAITH

Faith is always justified.*
Not faith in forms, which continue to shift and change,
But faith in Being, the essential quality of existence.
Faith is to trust that I don't have to do this alone.
Faith is to believe and know that I have access to help from an intelligence more expanded than my own.
Faith is always justified because I'm never not part of oneness.
Faith is always justified because Spirit is animating this form,
And Spirit is the connection point with God.
Life leaves many challenges at our feet.   Faith asks the question, "Would you face these alone, or would you receive assistance?"
And the truth of things is that we can never be alone, except from within the confines of a confused mind.
This very moment we are accessing Spirit.
So we make prayers, meditate upon the Self, and begin to see for ourselves if there is something incorruptible here.
To see for ourselves if there is an unshakable love we can rest in.
To see if there is a sun that will clear all darkness from our minds.
Until we see the sun for ourselves, we hold our candle of faith.

*Line from A Course In Miracles

PURPOSE

Purpose is simple. There is no grandiosity in purpose. It is a reflection of a commitment that we have made, and a demonstration of our faith.

Purpose is always simple. It is not a telling of what one intends to accomplish. Nor is it an anchor to be held down by.

Purpose is the distillation of our commitment, and always to one of two things: life or death.

Commitment to life means taking on the task of learning unconditional love. Both to love unconditionally and that I am loved unconditionally. Being committed to life directs us towards healing and wholeness, and leads to the gradual restoration of the pathways to infinite communication.

Commitment to death means to cherish punishment and condemnation. It is to believe that guilt is important and powerful and that love is weak. Commitment to death is the self-administered curse from which many of us are waking up from.

Purpose unites all of us in our commitment to either life or death. Every person who's committed to life is joined. In our joining, we create a unified field. And what arises out of this field will be nothing short of miraculous.

NON-ATTACHMENT

The principle of non-attachment rests on an obvious and simple truth: that the forms of this world cannot stand for long. However, the life that they hold, the energy of life, is what translates from form to form. So we hold lightly our attachments to the forms while honoring and bowing to the life they host.

You could say that non-attachment is a way of looking past the surface, of piercing through the transient elements of life to join with the timeless energies therein contained. A way of clearing the brush aside to step onto the spiritual ground of life.

This does not mean that we avoid life. Quite the opposite, in fact. We embrace life and everything that arises here. We accept that we do not control the outcomes of our life situations. We live each moment fully- letting our hearts be vulnerable, feeling the depth of our love, and at times, the depth of our pain. Because we practice non-attachment, we do not avoid pain, and we do not chase after love. We meet with life right where it is, right where we are. This takes courage, and the capacity for this level of space holding is developed over time.

An exercise to try:

Sit quietly for a minute or two grounding, breathing and sinking into presence.

Then think of something you feel quite attached to- a person, a place, or perhaps a pet.

Begin to think of all the qualities you love about it- its gentleness, its generosity, its beauty, etc. Pausing to let yourself feel whatever feelings accompany these thoughts, probably warm and happy feelings.

Then think of one or two things about it that you don't quite like. Perhaps it peed on the carpet. Or once you fell and scraped your knee there. Pausing to notice the feelings that come up.

Now, as you hold the image of this one in your mind, say goodbye to it. Release it. Look at it as though this is the last time you'll see it, and say goodbye. You may be tempted to imagine their response. But do your best to stay with your feeling.

Pause and hang out in this space for a few minutes. The space of letting go. We are not letting the thing go, we are letting go our ideas about it. We are letting it be free instead of overlaying it with images and interpretations from our minds. This is freedom for both self and other. This is non-attachment.

WONDER

Wonder is the most important quality of the spiritual aspirant. Wonder is to actively not know.

Wondering at something is to approach it with an honest openness. An openness freed from agenda and assumption. This openness lays the groundwork for the receptivity necessary to hear the subtle messages from Spirit.

Wonder helps us to cultivate the essential quality of the Witness that says, nothing needs to happen.

Wonder keeps us honest because it is the offspring of innocence. To wonder means, I still don't know everything. It means I'm open to being shown the way.

Innocence produces honesty because the innocent have no need to be dishonest. To wonder is, therefore, a pathway to a direct experience of unbroken innocence.

"I don't know" are holy words.
"I wonder" is a precious statement.

Say these words often, and when you do,
Speak them with dignity.
Develop a sense of reverence for each new moment.
Revel in the not knowing of what comes next.
Taste the sweetness of innocent wonder,
And trust that this is you at your most authentic.

THANK YOU

If you've made it this far, I must thank you for your persistence. I would also encourage you to re-read this book occasionally to see how you are integrating the information. With most spiritual texts, it is common to experience them differently after taking some time away to integrate. It could be like experiencing it for the first time, only this time, understanding the materials at a deeper level.

I bow to you in your inherent wisdom. I lift you up in your inherent value. I stand with you in the spirit of oneness. Let us stand together with dignity, displaying our hearts, listening to our inner guidance, and trusting that we are enough.

This world is not composed of separate objects bumping into each other, but of connected elements being drawn in together. That you found this book is no accident. That you read this far is not by chance. See for yourself if you can feel the hum of life that connects me to you at this very moment. We are never separate no matter what the world tells us. Life remains as an undivided whole. Touch that sense of knowing, and you will find the Witness standing there with you.

THE WITNESS

IMAGE INDEX

www.ingramcontent.com/pod-product-compliance
Lightning Source LLC
LaVergne TN
LVHW051418080426
835508LV00022B/3152